Fractured

STEAMY PARANORMAL &
SCI-FI ROMANCE

POETRY

A Collection of Poems for the Lovelorn

S.V. Brosius

S.V. Brosius

Cover design and illustrations by: Patty Ringgenberg

CONTENTS

FOREWORD

As I was writing this fifth collection of poetry, my intention was to capture at least a handful of the many emotions that come with being in love or desiring love. Our souls are designed to be loved, and we never stop seeking it. Many sources of inspiration helped me create these poems. I am someone who enjoys categorizing things to keep myself organized, so that is why the poems are grouped together as they are.

My romance stories inspired several of the poems in this collection and I hope you will read them, if you haven't already. I am grateful to you for investing your time in my books and I hope you enjoy "Fractured."

When did my worth suddenly become

hinged on seeing that you liked my post?

When did my worth suddenly become

hinged on whether your story was about me?

When did my worth suddenly become

hinged on whether you leave me on

"Opened?"

You've become a social media monster

that is not self-aware.

The scars and damage you've caused

are way beyond repair.

Yet I crave the attention and desire your text,

always wondering what words will come

next.

IN THE SADDLE

It's a bright sunny day and the grass is green
everywhere.
You chose the gentlest horse from your
stables just for me.
I try to mount her without help but you
place your hands around my middle.
My leg swings over the brown leather saddle
and I'm exactly where I'm supposed to be.

You climb in the saddle behind me, so I won't
fall.
I let you wrap your arms around my waist.
The scent of your cologne makes me pull you
closer.

We take off at a trot, then gallop to make
haste.

Eager to get to our favorite spot by the river,

under the shade of a large elm tree,

where we will kiss and whisper our love so

sweetly

and plan for our future eventually.

AGAINST THE LOCKERS

As my back presses into the cold metal, I

enjoy your sweet kisses and gentle caresses.

The school day continues around me with all

its never-ending drama and messes.

My mind recalls the day so long ago,

when my year-long bully shoved me against

the lockers.

Gaining the upper hand was an impossible

thing to do.

The students did nothing but watch,

completely off their rockers.

It was you that stepped out of the heartless
crowd,

seeing me differently than everyone else did.

You cold cocking my tormentor was satisfying

and loud.

I met your gaze at first, then turned away and

hid.

Shame and embarrassment at being a victim

won.

You found me with no effort and told me he

was done.

I thanked you with a chaste hug, then

looked away and down.

You lifted my chin and frowned at my frown.

"Don't you know how pretty you are?"

"Don't you know I don't care about your

scar?"

A gentle kiss and lots of hugs later...

he tells everyone "I'm proud to date her."

THE NEW GUY

We passed in the hallway after my biology
class.
I noticed your curly hair and you noticed my
sass.

It's the end of the school year so how could I
miss
this very hot new guy who I definitely want to
kiss!

Prom is only a few weeks away I know.
I don't have a date, but I really want to go.

My bestie joins me as we head across the school.

I tell her about him as I try to stay cool.

She knows who he is and sends him a snap.

He sends one back wearing a baseball cap.

She shows me her phone and then I exclaim:

OMG I can't believe he's on the baseball team!

There's a game coming up in just a few days.

We agree to go and snack on pizza and Lay's.

The new guy is the best player out there!

Our team scores big and wins with fanfare.

I wait by the fence so I can congratulate him.

He walks by with a friend, and I hear his

name is Tim.

I shout out to Tim my kudos on his big win.

He looks at me with a megawatt grin.

I wait for him as the stands empty out.

He appears and asks me what this is about.

I give him a flirty smile and the appearance of

calm.

I casually ask if he would like to go to prom.

The megawatt grin is back on his face

as he tells me, "Anytime, anyplace!"

PROM NIGHT

The looming clouds won't dampen my spirit.

My heartbeat's so loud I'm surprised you
can't hear it.

Eager for my "High School Musical" dreams
to come true,

an evening with friends and dancing with
you.

We wear matching colors of silver and blue

as we pose for pictures and plan what to do.

A limo ride through the heart of our city is
nice,

then an upscale dinner of steak and fancy
rice.

We arrive in style at the prom with our
friends,

wishing this magical night never ends.

GHOSTED

We had the start of a special something, or
so I thought.
I feel like an unopened email or an unfinished
Insta post.
My corporeal self still walks among the halls,
my spiritual self haunts your memory like a
ghost.

Would it have been better if I had sent you
away?
Maybe tossed you a penny or a dime,
pretended you pissed me off
or that you were never worth my time?

Confusion clouds my vision of you with her

as you dine on lunchroom nuggets and fries.

There is no recognition when you look at me.

I can see nothing but vagueness in your eyes.

I wish I could forget our walks around the
track

or the Red Bull slushes after school.

You let me hang with your sporty friends

and made me feel important and cool.

I guess I'll never know why you chose me

or why I let you into my heart.

You took my pride and bent it in half

and that will always be the hardest part.

TOO SHY

I've written love poems in your honor
but you'll never read them because I'm too
shy.

I've screenshotted your picture a few times
but you'll never see them because I'm too
shy.

I've baked cookies with your name on them
but you'll never taste them because I'm too
shy.

I've made a playlist of your favorite songs

but you'll never hear them because I'm too shy.

I've crafted homemade bath salts with your cologne
but you'll never smell them because I'm too shy.

I've kept you in my prayers every night at bedtime
but you'll never know that because I'm too shy.

ESCAPE IN THE NIGHT

I don't know where you came from

but you save my life every night.

You're there waiting for me

after I get off work – a welcome sight.

My clothes smell of grease and onions

but you never complain or say a word.

I often ask why you even bother with me;

Your frequent reply is "Don't be absurd!"

"It's dark and unsafe for you this late.

I want to make sure you get home.

I know how you feel because I'm the same;

Wishing to get away from the pain and just
roam."

I feel a special connection with him,
like he gets me when no one else can.
The barrage of judgment stings from my
family
over my obsession with this one man.

I sit behind him on his turbo charged bike,
wrapping my arms around his waist.
We don't go to my house right away,
just a detour in the country without haste.

He holds my hand in his for a short quiet
walk.

I let him kiss me and hold me for a while.

I'm happy for a small moment in time.

His undivided attention always makes me

smile.

The escape in the night is over too quickly.

He drives me home at a leisurely pace.

We kiss good night and hold each other tight,

making my fragile little heart race.

He doesn't show up for the next few nights,

the absence worrying me to no end.

When he finally reappears and I hop on his

bike,

he takes a different route just around the

bend.

I ask him why he's been gone so long.

He says he doesn't want to hurt me.

I tell him I don't understand what he means.

He says he is going to leave me be.

My tears aren't enough to change his mind

as he drives me home in a hurry.

I beg him to explain so I can know why

but he drops me off and leaves in a flurry.

I cry for days but no one seems to care

as I wonder what happened to my hero.

I never see or hear from him again,

leaving me hollow and less than zero.

RIVER OF TEARS

It never ends, this flowing river of tears.

My eyes ache, my heart burns.

All I can do with these empty arms

is paddle my way through the pain of not

having you.

The crestfallen trees hover over my head,

dropping their leaves of shame on me.

They block the sun and make the air cold.

Will it always be like this now that

you're gone from my life?

I never thought you would leave me like this,

after everything we shared and all our

precious kisses.

My dreams of a future with you have turned

to stones -

stones that now live in the bottom of

this endless river of tears.

TO MATT

We found each other again after all these years!

I love your humor and your sweet quirky smile.

Your body has changed but who really cares?

This reunion has proved we can go the extra mile.

I cheered in silence for you at all the football games,

even though you didn't know I was there.

I didn't know that you were interested in me back then.

It wouldn't have changed anything; we couldn't have been a pair.

I'm so grateful to God for bringing me back to you.
If you want me to stay, that's what I want too.
We are having so much fun being together again:
My love for you will never end.

Your New/Almost Old Girlfriend,

Carly

(Inspired by "Reunion Rendezvous" from the book "Duality" by S.V. Brosius)

for the woman
who explores

COSMIC INTERFERENCE

Our paths crossed but we don't know why.

Some cosmic interference invaded our sky.

Two beings with shadows on their souls

brought together only as they play their

roles.

Caught in this universe we did not create,

sharing words and voice and maybe a little

faith.

Invisible strings that go beyond love or care,

kindred spirits with a soul connection to

share.

TO JED

I saw you first and don't you forget it.

Country roads won't get you very far.

Your pickup truck may be big and fast

but not as fast as my speedy blue car!

A heart of gold like yours is sweet,

despite your fits of rage once in a while.

I thought no one would ever tame me

but you fell for me and my style.

I want this life of wheat fields and farms

only if I can share it with you.

Your family will be mine and mine will be

yours:

You ask me and I will say I do.

Your big city girl always,

Lanie

(Inspired by "Country Roads" by S.V. Brosius)

CITY BEATS

Amid the pulse of rush hour traffic

while the sunrise streaks across the distant

horizon...

Through the haze of morning fog

and aromas of freshly brewed coffee...

My thoughts are only of you, my love.

Missing your presence, your laugh, your

smile;

Feeling the beat of my heart in a city of lost

souls...

My uniqueness against a dark sea of misery.

TO TONY

You found me just as I found you -

Two broken souls with nowhere to go.

Here in this magical world of mist

We shared a meal and then we kissed.

I had lost myself for way too long,

Thinking he was right and I was wrong.

You showed me how to find my voice

And that forgiveness is the only choice.

I love you,

Maizie

(Inspired by "Mountain Interlude" by S.V. Brosius)

MIRROR IMAGE

The woman you see every day at work is only

a mirror image of the woman she once was.

She's taken the love risk too many times,

dated the bad boy who crossed too many

lines,

flirted with the power suit who didn't like to

share,

kissed the auto mechanic who didn't seem to

care,

danced with the gigolo who had all the right

moves,

gambled with the player who didn't like to

lose…

The woman you see every day at work is only a mirror image of the woman she once was.

BARE

The bronzed Adonis is planting another tree next door.

His bare back glistens with tiny droplets as she watches his shoulder blades shift under his taut skin.

The dark-haired man is building a new shed next door.

His bare arms reveal thick cords of veins as she imagines the power in each strike of his hammer.

The charming neighbor is picking flowers from his garden next door.

His bare chest is solid muscle as she pretends

the fresh blooms nestled in his embrace are meant for her.

The blushing Venus is drinking coffee on her balcony next door.
Her bare lips blow across the mug as he watches the mesmerizing movement of her mouth as she sips.

The dark-haired woman is reading a book in her lounge chair next door.
Her bare fingers slowly turn the pages as he imagines the delicate touch of her skin on his.

The alluring neighbor is swimming in her pool next door.

Her bare legs kick and flex as he pretends the long, luscious limbs are wrapped around his torso.

Both are willing to love and to share,

wanting each other in mutual care,

needing to be bold...needing to be bare.

BLEED

My veins bleed your final words of goodbye,
staining the cement below me with splatters
of crimson pain.
Your veins bleed my pleas of longing,
dripping through the cracks never to be seen
again.
My heart pumps you in while your heart
pumps me out.
Seeping blood appears when I don't want it
to, bringing the pain of my love for you in
vivid technicolor before my eyes.

MOONLIGHT

My garden of blooms takes on an ethereal beauty under the cool warmth of your moonlight. You are the dark angel that my soul longs for. I can barely contain my desire as I wait for you in the shadows. When I finally see the sparkling green of your eyes in the black night, my heart leaps for joy. You open your arms to beckon me forth as the moonlight glints off your perfect white fangs. I willingly want to flow into you through the gift of my nourishing blood. You cling to me as I surrender to you with the promise of secret desires and unearthly bliss.

We own the moonlight this night...and every night forever more.

TO CHASIS

What is it that you see in someone like me?

I can't offer you the one thing you seek.

You've unwrapped this sheltered young girl

and crafted a cultured rare pearl.

I don't deserve your love yet it's mine

forever.

You make me try and you make me better.

I worry for you in your battle of duality,

praying that you won't be the casualty.

Know that my love for you has no bounds.

I'm in love with a vampire as strange as that sounds.

Eternally yours,

Clare

(Inspired by "The Darkness of Day" by S.V. Brosius)

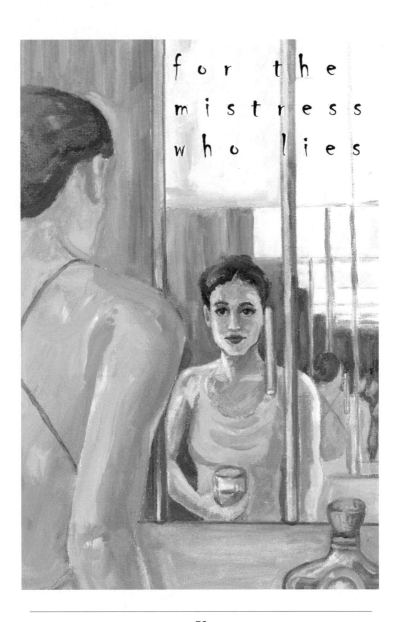

for the
mistress
who lies

UNATTAINABLE

Never in my wildest dreams did I plan to
meet someone like you.
The universe has its way of placing us in each
other's orbs out of the blue.

I want to be with you, you want to be with
me,
but the unattainable you and the
unattainable me know in our hearts that we
can never be.

My heart holds you in deep folds of sincerity
when I say to you that I wish you could see
I cannot be bound by this lack of clarity.

Your world is not where I expect to see

a true and honest life for me.

FORBIDDEN LONGING

Why do I miss you when you were never
mine?
A risk, a dare, a temptation to cross the line.

Miss Swift warns us of illicit affairs,
bringing pain and loathing and star-crossed
stares.

We cannot speak and we cannot touch,
knowing it would only hurt that much.

I look for your presence in the haze of my
memory
when we saw each other with unabashed
reverie.

You with your movie star good looks were no match for me.

I tried to ignore you, but our meeting was meant to be.

It was love at first sight for you but not for me.

I knew once I let you inside my heart, I would never be free.

If only I had known about her in the first place.

You lied and hid away her beautiful face.

The fates are cruel and shameless with the
lovelorn fools,

breaking the ones who follow all the rules.

I want to see you be happy with your girl one
day,

but I'm a jealous woman and will never be
okay.

THE HOTEL ROOM

Number 216 houses many dirty secrets.

He pays for the room, she makes it divine.

A tray of delectable pastries and fruit

complement the bottle of very fine wine.

The two have been meeting this way for

years;

a lover's escape from the chains of their

rings.

Their kids don't know and never will at this

rate.

They are too busy with their lives and other

things.

The whirlpool tub is filled and ready for use.

Strawberry scented bubbles permeate the

air.

The two take their pleasure with wild

abandon,

never noticing the suspiciousness already

there.

Clothed in matching robes, the lovers are

faced with the truth.

Standing in room 216 face to face with hurt-

filled eyes,

he watches his wife cry as she watches her

husband seethe.

"Apologies are hollow," they say with collective sighs.

Everyone finds their way home somehow, locking the secrets of 216 away one last time. The real world holds problems that are too impossible to solve as the lovers become strangers and pretend to be fine.

Their good thing together wasn't so good for anyone else.
Fleeting moments now exist only in their memories.
Spouses that had been their best friends have become nothing more than frenemies.

CLOSE MY EYES

I don't want to see the anguish I've caused
you.
I don't want to hear the scolding I deserve.
I don't want to feel the burn of your grip.
Close my eyes.

I don't want to know the number of times
you covered for me.
I don't want to smell the roses I didn't earn.
I don't want to taste your salty tears when I
try to kiss it better.
Close my eyes.

The concentrated swirl of foreboding and
guilt
colors my vision of the wall I have built.

Your anger will only fester and rise.
Please, my love, just close my eyes.

THE WEDDING GUEST

You had the nerve to invite me to your
wedding!
You have no idea where this will be heading!

She chose my favorite flowers for her
bouquet...
and my favorite wedding colors for her
special day.

As I watch you waiting at the altar for your
bride
my heartbroken expression is one I cannot
hide.

What am I doing here when I should have
stayed away?
Was I hoping you would learn to see things
my way?

TO KING ARRIUS

You courted me, married me, and made me
leave my home.
Promises of prosperity and happiness filled
me with hope.

It started with longing glances from you to
me.
I wanted your touch and your love so badly.

But you built a wall between us and left me
alone,
forcing me into another man's world.

He gives me purpose and wants a life
together,
so farewell, my king and good riddance
forever.

Cordially,

Her Majesty Queen Yennia

(inspired by "The Prisoner's Mark" by S.V. Brosius & Lindsey Hartford)

THE PLAYER

I knew better than to fall for your charms.

Instead, I practically ran into your arms.

With your perfect pearly whites

and ego at new heights,

The player in you keeps me on a string,

dangling promises of everything.

I'll miss our talks as if you were my friend.

I know what's best for me in the end.

You're every woman's dream man,

seducing every innocent you can.

It was fun while it lasted, I guess...

You can keep the brand-new dress.

WILL I EVER SEE YOU AGAIN?

You are a man of duty and obligation.

I am a woman of passion and art.

A seductive spell wrapped around us one
night,

holding us together until we had to part.

I knew you were shipping out to foreign
lands,

brave and handsome in your uniform of blue.

You said I was pretty and full of charm,

and staying with me was all you wanted to
do.

I savored every letter you sent me,

as I hope you did mine.

We talked of weather and food

and architectural design.

What we didn't write was the truth about us

and all the reasons we should have ran.

How you have another waiting at home

while I am betrothed to an unlovable man.

It's not just this and distance that separates

us,

it's family, it's jobs, it's unspoken confessions.

Our one night together was never enough,

despite the promises of darkness's

protections.

So, remember me fondly as I'll remember you.

Don't ever lose that noble sparkle in your eye.

I can't stop wondering if I will see you again.

I know the answer, but my dream will never die.

for the wife
who tries

BEDROOM TEARS

Why must you confess your misdeeds for the
day
as I lay upon my soft and fluffy pillow?
Bound together by all the wrong things to
say,
wondering where my heart is supposed to go.

I became your confessional somewhere along
the way
as I focus on the feel of our silky sheets.
Tears spill over to try and convey...
silent pain is my greatest of feats.

LOSE MYSELF IN YOU

A simple choice to lose myself in you would set the love I have in my heart on a flight to endless skies. I wouldn't need to breathe or bear the weight of earthly responsibilities. My eyes would only see the blue light of your adoring gaze. My body would only feel the caress of your gentle fingertips. My soul would only feel the beauty of our love.

An easy way to live and dream.
An easy way to hide in the folds of surreal bliss.
Closer to eternity...further from the ticking clock of truth.

THE BROKEN WHISKEY BOTTLE

Amber liquid covers the cream-colored wall and the hardwood floors beneath. Shards of glass litter the room, as sharp as the words my tongue lashed at you.

I'm done waiting for the apologies that will never escape your lips.

I'm done pining for the lovemaking that you have given to someone else.

I'm done drowning my agony in the warmth of a liquor haze.

Call it an epiphany or the release of all that is vile in my fractured heart...

What we had is destroyed, just like the broken whiskey bottle that missed you by one little inch.

CARRY

Is it wrong for me to be tired of the carry?

Is it wrong for me to feel forced to make merry?

I carried our babies from the womb to the arms.

I carried the burdens of financial alarms.

I work myself to the point of fatigue.

I do not foresee relief or reprieve.

It's not a good day for me to carry.

Life is not my friend but an adversary.

Black clouds gather above my soul,

a rain of depression their dastardly goal.

My solitary island lies in a sea of ice.

A tropical heat wave about now would be
nice.

COLD MORNINGS

Winter is tortuous without you here.

My feet are icy, not to mention my rear!

I just came in from letting our dog out,

loving her company despite her chilly snout.

The heater is on the fritz once more,

but you're not here to fix it like before.

Our bills are piling up with no end in sight.

I'm working my tail off trying to make it right.

You left me with heart wounds that will never

heal.

I want to forget you're gone; pretend it isn't real.

You didn't leave me much, but I still feel your love...
as you float carefree among the stars up above.

DINNER FOR ONE

The candles brighten the dining room to full
effect.
The linens add a touch of color and class.
The silver utensils are polished and ready.
The stemware is imported and made of real
glass.

I shopped and cooked and baked all day,
anxious to do something nice for you.
I know how hard you work at the office;
planning a romantic dinner is the least I can
do.

The clock ticks the minutes as the candlelight
dims.
You're not answering my texts at all.
I wonder who made you stay this time,
or if I dare to even call.

My stomach is grumbling so I go ahead and
eat
as the candlelight continues to dim.
You still aren't home when I finish
and I wonder "what shall I do about him?"

I crawl in bed and leave everything for the
pretend maid.
Then, I hear him open the door and come in.

A perfume that isn't mine lingers in our
room;

he gets in the shower, and I let my tears win.

SHARING OUR WORLDS

You love horror movies, and I don't at all.

I love musicals and you'd just rather not.

I enjoy easy-to-prepare meals,

while you'd rather avoid the Crock-Pot.

You want to go camping outdoors,

I prefer to hang out at home.

You want to take road trips,

I'd rather stay local to roam.

Our kids enjoy pushing our buttons,

you know how they can be.

I let you deal with the personality issues that

are you,

you let me deal with the personality issues that are me.

Sharing our worlds is fun and worth the effort.
Our individual identities make this marriage strong.
As our unconditional love grows between us, how could anything ever go wrong?

We don't have to give up what we love to do, accommodating for each other is the best way.
Expanding our interests is healthy and mature.
Let's get started...what do you say?

MARRIAGE TIES

Remember when you proposed to me?
I knew my life would change that day.
Life takes turns that no one can predict;
you were with me all the way.

I lost my dad, and soon after my mom.
The burden of their finances all my own.
You held me through the tears and the grief;
my love for you has grown.

Your dad grew ill, and your grandma died.
The family was saddened in shock.
I comforted you the best I knew how,
trying hard to be your solid rock.

Our marriage ties us together forever,

a precious bond that no one can sever.

GLIMPSE OF HEAVEN

Every featherlight touch of your hand,

every time you help me to stand...

is a glimpse of Heaven.

Every moment we spend in an embrace,

every mutual smile upon our face...

is a glimpse of Heaven.

Every kiss that sweeps us away,

every word of love that we say...

is a glimpse of Heaven.

Every thought of how our future will be,

every memory of you being with me...

is a glimpse of Heaven.

SUNLIGHT ON THE WATER

You found my deep fathomless ocean

once upon a nighttime swim.

I didn't believe you were real at first,

that you were you and not him.

My chaotic waves didn't force you out,

just made you plunge even deeper.

As my dark waters became a lighter blue,

I soon realized that you were a keeper.

I used to think I had to find a peaceful shore,

a place to feel the sun upon my skin.

But you became my sunlight on the water,

and made me happier than I've ever been.

It is under the gaze of the full moon that I
flourish.

It is under the haze of your unbridled love
that I flourish.

It is under the days of friendly smiles and
camaraderie that I flourish.

It is under the rays of sunshine that I flourish.

It is under the daze of soul enriching beauty
that I flourish.

It is under the maze of a God blessed life that
I flourish.

PINK SKIES

You have brought pink skies into my world,

the sweetest color to mask the gray.

Your laugh and your charm make me smile,

floating the darkness away.

You hold my hand in the warmth of your

own,

leading me to that comfortable spot.

The moment your lips are on mine,

I realize that I'm forever caught.

You let me cry on your shoulder when I'm

sad,

never making me feel like a fool.

Your gentle touch on my skin keeps me calm.

You want honesty, that's your only rule.

I want us to share our dreams together,

to keep pink skies in our world forever.

CHEERS

We celebrate our married years together

with cheers;

me with my margs and you with your beers.

We held each other through the fears,

and suffered through the tears,

brought up two humans with fun and jeers.

We celebrate our married years together

with cheers.

LOVE BEYOND

Our love has grown beyond the bounds of
rafters and brick,
deeper than the life trials through thin and
thick,
fuller than the jobs and volunteer work that
we do,
richer than any inheritance, too.

Bigger than the pride we have for our
daughter and son,
sweeter than all our times of good fun.
Our love is blessed, our love is beyond.

STAYING TOGETHER

This love is forged in so many things

as I stare in awe at our wedding rings.

The barely there kisses and hugs in a rush

are just as important as the ones that make

us blush.

Moments when we hang out and talk as

friends

form the lifelong bond that never ends.

Sometimes we drift toward a major

distraction

but it is always followed by a rekindled
attraction.

Knowing how we saw each other through
life's tears
ends the confusion and calms the fears.

This love is forged in so many things
as I stare in awe at our wedding rings.

ACKNOWLEDGEMENT

Thank you to Patty Ringgenberg for the beautiful artwork that graces the cover and the sections of "Fractured." I am grateful for our continued partnership in creating poetry books together.

Thank you to my family and friends, as well as my co-workers for their continued support.

Thank you to the other indie authors I have had the pleasure to meet either in person or online. You all inspire me to keep writing no matter what.

REVIEWS

PLEASE LEAVE A REVIEW OF THIS BOOK ON AMAZON, GOODREADS, OR BOOKBUB. IT HELPS ME AND OTHER READERS SO MUCH!

If you would rather email me directly with your review so I can put it on my website, please send it to: svbrosiusauthor@gmail.com. **If you want to be anonymous - no problem!** Just let me know that in your email.

THANK YOU!

BOOKS BY THIS AUTHOR

PARANORMAL ROMANCE BOOKS

Mountain Interlude

https://a.co/d/9jn3On6

Deep in the mountains of Colorado stands an old house shrouded in mist. A lonely, divorced woman will come face to face with the attractive man who owns the property. She will find herself in a world of paranormal mystery: a place where the lost are taken care of, the injured are healed, and time stands still.

*E-BOOK IS FREE FOR S.V. BROSIUS NEWSLETTER SUBSCRIBERS. SIGN UP HERE: https://www.svbrosiusauthor.com/home%23 newsletter-sign-up

The Darkness of Day

https://books2read.com/u/m2qPJr

Her journey into adulthood was just beginning. A vampire hero changed her life forever. This is Clarabella's story.

Nothing extraordinary ever happened to Clarabella Moore...until the night a vampire came to her rescue. But Chasis was no ordinary vampire. A member of the Brotherhood of Sacred Light, Chasis has a duty to protect Clarabella. However, his infatuation awakens her to danger and a world of not only vampires, but other supernatural beings as well. Suddenly, Clarabella's world is anything but dull.

But when a mysterious villain threatens to expose the Brotherhood's most prized secret, Clarabella has no choice but to go along for the ride and experience the romance she has always wanted with the hero of her dreams.

A world where her sexual desires come to life and her faith is put to the test.

POETRY/ROMANCE SHORT STORY BOOKS

Duality

https://a.co/d/5nnmfUg

Past and present fuse together in this collection of poetry and romance short stories written to expose the light and dark side in all of us.

Featuring:
The Cupid Florist
(a clean romance)

The Electric Highway
(a forced proximity sci-fi romance)

The New Husband
(a forced proximity sci-fi horror romance)

Reunion Rendezvous
(a sweet second chance romance)

KINDLE VELLA STORIES (SOON TO BE EBOOKS AND PAPERBACKS)

The Prisoner's Mark

https://www.amazon.com/kindle-vella/story/B0CVZYR5C1

The new queen of Kenimo has succumbed to the roguish charms of her pirate prisoner. Little does she know that her decision to help him escape will trigger a powerful curse that will haunt them wherever they go.

Co-Written with Lindsey Hartford.

Escape with Me

https://www.amazon.com/kindle-vella/story/B0D8Z1YVTX

I have no memory of my life before this. My current residence is a dank prison cell. I have no idea how I got here, but I know the reason I am here: my blood. Now, my only hope of survival lies with my captor's human servant. The only link to my past. The only human decency I am allowed to experience. He cares for me. I need his help to escape.

Country Roads

https://www.amazon.com/kindle-vella/story/B0CMQF93ZC

A big city girl with no plans for her future finds herself in the quiet wheat fields and dirt roads of Kansas. Will her curious nature and lust for life manage to win over the intriguing cowboy that crosses her path?

Harbinger's Princess

https://www.amazon.com/kindle-vella/story/B0CCM9SWLW

What mysteries and temptations await young Rayanne as she travels the galaxy in a haunted spaceship?

POETRY BOOKS

Water Colored World

https://books2read.com/u/3GpLDp

Explore the power and emotion of nature's most diverse element: water. Raindrops, snowflakes, oceans, or ice...we can see reflections of ourselves in this collection of poetry.

Earthbound Journeys

https://books2read.com/u/b5Wl8p

From the trials of motherhood, the appreciation of nature, exploring romantic fantasy, and embracing faith through the loss of family - this is a poetic journal of survival. 1st Place Poetry Winner - 2022 Stellar Book Awards.

On Her Side of the Cosmos

https://books2read.com/u/bxNpXk

From the innocence of first love to first heartbreak - this is the poetic journey of evolving love from the romantic perspectives of a young woman as she grows into maturity. Elements of science fiction and faith round out this selection of poems.

WAYS TO FOLLOW S.V. BROSIUS

Visit www.svbrosiusauthor.com and sign up for the FREE newsletter for information on the latest releases, ongoing Kindle Vella stories, exclusive behind-the-book author blog, free short stories, and deleted scenes!

FOR ALL SOCIAL MEDIA LINKS:

https://linktr.ee/svbrosius

Made in United States
Troutdale, OR
01/18/2025

28091563R00062